GOLDEN GEMS
OF
POETRY

BY

BETTY ELLER

Library of Congress Control Number: 2009928557

ISBN 978-0-9822230-3-1

All Scripture quotes are from the King James Bible.

Address All Inquiries To:
THE OLD PATHS PUBLICATIONS, Inc.
142 Gold Flume Way
Cleveland, Georgia, 30528
U.S.A.

Web: www.theoldpathspublications.com
E-mail: TOP@theoldpathspublications.com

1.0

THIS BOOK IS DEDICATED TO

JESUS CHRIST

MY LORD AND SAVIOUR,
MY PROPHET, PRIEST AND KING.

ALSO, THIS BOOK IS DEDICATED TO

TOM ELLER

MY KIND, DEVOTED AND THOUGHTFUL
HUSBAND, WHO SO WILLINGLY
ENCOURAGED AND HELPED FULFILL
THIS WORK.

To:

Albert + Martha Jean

Best Wishes
to

Two Special People!!

Betty Ellen

FOREWORD

NOTE FROM THE AUTHOR

Early in life, while growing up near Waynesboro, Pennsylvania, words started to flow and I found myself placing them on paper with pen and ink. Little did I realize that these thoughts and words would continue to flow. After marriage to my beloved husband, Tom, we lived in Modesto, California where many of these poems were written. In 1985, we moved to the peace and solitude of the Northeast Georgia Mountains, near Cleveland, Georgia, giving me the inspiration for many more poems. We photographed the beautiful scenery and peacefulness of these mountains, which have been used for most illustrations.

Our two lovely daughters, Laura and Carla along with their husbands, Dean and Ryan were dear encouragers and supporters. And I can't forget our precious grandchildren, Sheri', Jeff, LoriAnn and Logan, shocked that Grandma could write a book.

Currently, we continue to call these hills of North Georgia our home....

Friends ask us why we're here --
      And we say --
We don't know why we're here,
      Except,
That the peace and tranquility
      Of these hills,
Affect the peace and tranquility
      Of our lives,
It is here we can
      Cry with the rain;
      Laugh with the wind;
      Or float with the clouds.
Here we can surround our lives
      With the sounds of these hills,
      Or die by the silence of peace.

It is here where we can lift up our eyes
      Unto these hills,
And it is here where our help comes
      From the Lord;
For He shall preserve our souls
      From this time forth,
      And even forevermore.

TO GOD BE THE GLORY

These lines which have been written
Weren't written for honor and fame,
And I ask that all of your gratitude
Isn't given unto my name.

For I'm merely a simple instrument
That God has placed on earth,
And if, you too, will examine yourself,
You will find a talent that's worth,
Sharing with others around you
With the help of our "ALMIGHTY GOD"
For we each are merely an instrument,
To help lighten the pathway we trod.

Betty Eller

Ecclesiastes 3::22 "Wherefore I perceive that there is nothing better, than that a man should rejoice in his own works; for that is his portion; for who shall bring him to see what shall be after him?"

TABLE OF CONTENTS

Deuteronomy 28:3-6 "Blessed shat thou be in the city, and blessed shalt thou be in the field. Blessed shall be the fruit of thy body, and the fruit of thy ground, and the fruit of thy cattle, the increase of thy kine, and the flocks of thy sheep. Blessed shall be thy basket and thy store. Blessed shat thou be when thou comest in, and blessed shat thou be when thou goest out."

SECTION I

CHRIST

First Presbyterian Church, Clarkesville, GA

Colossians 1:27   "To whom God would make known what *is* the riches of the glory of this mystery among the Gentiles; which is Christ in you, the hope of glory:"

THE ROCK OF AGES

Lord, we know that we are living
In a time of restlessness;
Raging waves and tempest beating,
With strong winds of dreadfulness.
How our hearts so oft grow weary,
As the waves rush wild and high;
Beating on the rocks so swiftly,
Yet we know that Thou art nigh!

Help us to endure these moments,
Keep us safe within Thine arms.
For we know the "Rock of Ages,"
Is secure from all alarm.
Fill our hearts with thoughts of Jesus,
Of His presence and His love;
May we feast on words that promise
Life eternal high above.

Help us to be kind and loyal,
To obey, with love and praise;
Then when fury and frustrations
Seem to swell and seem to raise;
May we find ourselves well anchored
To the solid "Rock of Life,"
Ever guarded and protected
From the howling storms of strife.

Anna Ruby Falls

PRECIOUS ECHOS

There's a beautiful city
In a beautiful place,
Called Heaven where eternal
Sweet glories will shine.
The saints of all ages will walk
The streets of pure gold,
And we'll hear precious echoes
From Jesus "You're Mine!"

Oh to walk the streets of
The purest gold by His side,
And to bask in His presence
Forever we'll find,
That it was worth every moment
When tried by the fire,
As we hear precious echoes
From Jesus "You're Mine!"

There the saints of all ages,
And our friends gone before
Will sit with our Master
And Eternally dine;
We will sing hallelujah,
Oh the rock we have found,
While we hear precious echoes
From Jesus "You're Mine!"

Corinth Baptist Church

THE LAMBS

So often we're told
That the lambs in the fold
Will need a little more care.
Directing their feet,
Into ways that will keep,
Lambs from wandering somewhere.

It's easy to think
As one makes a quick wink,
All's safe in the little flock.
But let's look again,
Without a slight grin,
Of all the dangerous knocks.

Our duty is great
And there's no time to wait,
If we want the lambs secure.
We must use "God's" arms,
To prevent them from harm
And safety will be more sure.

Dr. Lott's Lambs

RIVER OF LIFE

The river of life continues to flow,
As time passes rapid and free;
Each soul has the choice to choose his own
    course,
As the river flows constantly.

So gentle it seems, while rolling downstream
'Midst waters so calm and serene;
What blessed delight, to drift with no fight,
Creating a pacified scene.

But friend, have you thought, while drifting
    along,
Where the trends of currents may lead?
Your soul could be lost, tormented and
    tossed,
In currents of agonized speed.

For it takes a man most willing to stand
The currents that forcefully flow;
Indeed it is rough — the rapids are tough,
While the winds continue to blow.

But never give up — each rapid you climb,
Leads into God's Kingdom above;
Your soul will be blessed — forever to rest,
In the quiet pools of His love.

Below Anna Ruby Falls

HEAVEN'S HALL OF FAME

We're traveling to a city
Where we'll find a Hall of Fame;
Written in Golden Letters,
Will be God's chosen names.

Throughout all generations
God's recorded every name;
Worthy of Golden Letters,
In Heaven's Hall of Fame.

Ah! There in Heaven's City
Not a soul can mar your name;
Betrayal and deception
Aren't in God's Hall of Fame.

Untruthfulness, self-seeking,
And powers of selfish gain;
Will never be recorded
In Heaven's Hall of Fame.

Colorful Graffiti,
Degrading any name;
Can't block out Golden Letters
In Heaven's Hall of Fame.

Purified and molded,
Tried by fires of flame;
Make up the Golden Letters
In Heaven's Hall of Fame.

Refined, Polished, Recorded,
Will be God's chosen names;
Carved out of Golden Letters
In Heaven's Hall of Fame.

THE SHIP

In our life span we viewed a ship
Go sailing o'er the sea;
Inside we noticed many souls,
Content and so happy.

We watched that ship for several years,
Just gliding peaceably;
Was not a wave she could not crest,
She sailed so swift and free.

And every time we viewed that ship,
We heard a gentle plea;
The Captain of that very ship
Said, "COME and FOLLOW me."

At last, we too, got in the ship,
With waters calm and clear;
We sailed and sailed and sailed away,
Without a single fear.

But ah! The weather made a change,
Clouds formed within the skies;
Swift currents formed from little waves,
With torrents swift to rise.

And now we find the ship we joined
Just tossing to and fro;
Her rudder bent, yet on she sails,
In seas of troubled woe.

The waters rough! The waves are high!
We're banged and bruised within!
Yet still we hear that gentle voice,
So calm and smooth again.

"Have Faith - Have Faith!" the Captain
cries,
"Why are ye fearful now?"
"Walk on by Faith and not by sight" ---
We paused upon the bow.

And somehow, thru the darkest storm,
We viewed a ray of light;
We looked beyond and there we saw
A place of pure delight.

Again the Captain gently spoke,
"I'm with you 'til the end';
I will not leave you comfortless" ---
And then we smiled again.

WHAT DO WE NEED?

We don't need a face full of passion,
Carved out of imported gold,
We don't need the arms of an idol,
Wide open – so eager – to hold.

We don't need a path in a forest
With a cross at the end of the way,
We don't even need a white chapel
With soft padded alters to pray.

We just need the face of our JESUS,
Carved out of the spirit so true,
We just need the arms of our Saviour
Outstretched – while inviting us through.

We just need a path that is narrow,
To keep us from wandering astray,
We need power to deny ourselves –
That's the cross we'll carry each day.

We just need our secretive closet,
No carpet – He'll still hear above,
'Cause we are nothing but old timers
Just living from God's simple love.

Path to DeSoto Falls

SECTION II

CALVARY

Grace Calvary Episcopal Church, Clarkesville, GA

Luke 23:33 "And when they were come to the place, which is called Calvary, there they crucified him, and the malefactors, one on the right hand, and the other on the left."

THE EXISTING MOB

An angry mob once took our Lord
And led Him up Calvary's Hill;
While casting lots they spit on Him,
And Yet He remained calm and still.

The years have come - The years have gone
Since our Saviour was crucified;
While mocking Him they pierced His side
And anxiously watched as He died.

Could it be possible today
That part of the mob still exists?
Yes! We can hurt Him yet today
Without crosses, stones or a fist.

The sudden slip of our own tongue,
Or an evil thought passing by;
Lustfulness with wrath and strife
Are the ways we can crucify.

Let's not be part of any mob
Which leads Him to Calvary's Hill;
Instead be gentle, kind and good,
With meekness, be temperate and still.

Grace Calvary Episcopal Church, Clarkesville, GA

BETRAYAL

They led Him through a dark betrayal
So difficult to face;
They tortured Him with agony
Beyond the human race.
They led Him to the slaughter
As a lamb, so cruel and cold;
They spit, They kicked, They beat, They
    bruised,
They even pierced - we're told.

THEY — were His own who turned their
    backs
With uncontrolled control;
THEY — once were followers who agreed
But somehow lost their goal.
THEY- once were His that turned on Him,
Betrayed - receiving not;
THEY - walked with Him along the way,
Then suddenly forgot.

Could this be us? Or even you?
How solemnly we plea;
For in this day of grace we find
All followers don't agree.
Could the betrayal we seem to face
Be just a stubborn will
That should be slaughtered, left to bleed
Upon a rugged hill?

CALVARY

You've never been to Calvary
Unless you suffer pain;
Of grief and disappointments
That rend your heart in twain.

You've never been to Calvary
Unless you suffer loss;
From howling winds around you,
While billows roar and toss.

You've never been to Calvary
Unless you truly mourn;
And feel the shame and sorrow
Of souls, lost and forlorn.

You've never been to Calvary
Unless you've hung your head;
Stretched your hand — in total loss,
And somehow softly said...

"Commend my Spirit in Thy Hands
And Crucify my Will;
Forgive, Forgive, Dear Father,
Until Thy Plan's fulfilled."

Grace Calvary Episcopal Church, Clarkesville, GA

SCARS

When we stand before our Saviour
And we meet Him face to face;
All our records will be open
Regardless of our race.

All our trophies and our medals
And the ribbons we have won,
Won't be recognized in Heaven
For all that we have done.

But it'll be the scars we're wearing
That have pierced our very side;
Which will be revealed in Heaven,
And this, we cannot hide.

All our wounds and disappointments,
And our saddened, broken hearts,
Be we crippled, bruised or beaten,
Whatever was our part.

Will be souvenirs and keep-sakes,
Which have scarred our very soul;
For these spiritual indictments
Have kept us pure and whole.

So frown not at disappointments,
Which will oft create great scars;
Because when we meet our Maker --
Scars tell Him what we are.

"Except I shall see in his hands the print of the nails, and put my finger into the print of the nails, and thrust my hand into his side, I will not believe."   St. John 20:25

FORGIVENESS

One of the greatest blessings we have,
And one that is oft overlooked,
Is the "forgiving" power we have,
It's written in God's Holy Book.

A power to use time after time,
As we "give," forgetting our will;
Limits are endless, "give" on and on,
Again and again, even still.

And when we "forget" as we "forgive,"
We often "get" more than we "give;"
Like blessings of peace, blessings of love,
Enhancing the life which we live.

Clarkesville, GA

HE OPENED NOT HIS MOUTH

He was brought as a lamb to the slaughter,
Was despised and rejected of men;
Afflicted and wounded, bruised and oppressed,
Interceding for all of our sins.

Thus should we find this example to be,
A true pattern designed for His own;
As we suffer to pay the price of pain,
Our Saviour so gently has sown.   *ISAIAH 53*

Grace Calvary Episcopal Church, Clarkesville, GA

SECTION III

LOVE, PEACE, FAITH, TRUTH, WISDOM

Leona Lane, Cleveland, GA

Jude 1:2 *"Mercy unto you, and peace, and love, be multiplied."*

LOVE IS A GIFT

Every good gift and every perfect gift
Comes from the Father above,
And one of the greatest and one of the best
Are when folks are united in love.

A love that will grow and help to endure
The trials that so often we meet;
A love that is full of interest and concern,
To make life just a little more sweet.

A love that is shown by a kind little deed,
A nod or a friendly smile;
A love that unites two hearts into one,
When they're separated by so many miles.

It's definitely sure and it's certainly true,
All gifts are sent from above;
So generously given by the Father and Spirit,
To unite us in bonds of love.

Logan Filbrun and Jeff Bower

UNCONDITIONAL LOVE

When someone talks behind your back,
Or murmurs about what you say;
Sliding in and out, evading you,
From contact day to day.

Our earthly nature will rise up,
And it's quite hard not to fight back;
But men, we find, whom grace controls,
Will not step down that track.

God's love is unconditional,
And our love too, must be the same;
Regardless how we're treated here –
Our goal's not earthly fame.

So when attacks come from within,
Let's remain unconditional;
Just keep on loving more and more,
With a true committal.

GOD'S HAND OF FRIENDSHIP

There may be miles between us,
With rivers deep and wide,
But there's a "Hand" to guide us
That will keep us side by side.

It guides us through our daily walk,
Gives strength when e'er we tire;
It gives us comfort when depressed
And fills the needs we require.

It sends the little drops of rain,
The sunshine's golden rays,
It showers down each blessing
We receive from day to day.

With all of these dear blessings,
That come from God's own "Hand,"
How wide and deep are the rivers?
How long are the miles of land?

"Greater love hath no man than this, that a man lay down his life for his friends."   *St. John 15:13*

CARING FRIENDS

If nobody cared and nobody shared
And nobody thought of you,
If nobody laughed and nobody cried
And nobody's smiles were true;
The clouds would hang much lower
And the sun would shine so dim,
And the people just like you and me
Wouldn't even attempt to win;
The goal that awaits us tomorrow,
Perhaps just earning a friend
Who is always willing to strengthen
And lift us up again.
For life is a whole lot brighter
When a friend comes passing by;
Leaving a word of kindness
To lift our souls up high.
And life's just a little easier,
When we know that somebody cares,
And is waiting, ready to listen,
Or more than willing to share,
The little daily burdens
That grow heavy on our minds,
And seem to weight our shoulders down –
These friends are hard to find.

**LoriAnn Filbrun
Sheri' Bower**

FRIENDS

I wonder why God crossed our paths
And made our hearts grow dear;
I wonder why our inner souls
Trust each, without a fear.

I wonder why He made us friends,
I wonder why so much;
I wonder why our inner thoughts
Glow bright without a touch.

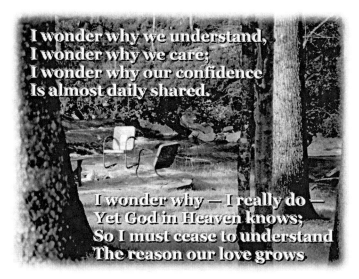

I wonder why we understand,
I wonder why we care;
I wonder why our confidence
Is almost daily shared.

I wonder why — I really do —
Yet God in Heaven knows;
So I must cease to understand
The reason our love grows

I just must thank our Lord above
For all His secret ways;
The friendship He's bestowed on us
Is worthy of all praise.

Oh may my actions and my thoughts,
With feeble words, I cry;
Accept these blessings while on earth,
'Til brighter bliss on high.

PEACE

Nothing in this old world of ours
Wherein we search, can find;
Such priceless virtue of its own —
And that's a peaceful mind.

No price can buy — no price can sell,
The bliss such peace bestows —
Nor can attempts begin to hide
A peace that warmly glows!

No words can e'er express such joy,
Nor comprehension find —
The swelling surge within one's soul,
And that's a peaceful mind.

Oh joy and bliss of peacefulness,
Quiet, serene and calm —
Fill every longing, waiting soul,
With Thy pure peaceful balm!

Path to Anna Ruby Falls

FAITH

It's gonna take faith --
And Lots of faith,
If we wanna pass the test...
For God in His infinite wisdom
Is separating grain from the rest.

It's gonna take faith --
And Lots of faith,
If we wanna withstand the storm...
For God in His infinite wisdom
Is checking each servant's form.

It's gonna take faith --
And Lots of faith,
If we wanna hold out to the end...
For God in His infinite wisdom
Is checking each current of wind.

It's gonna take faith --
And Lots of faith,
'Til we cross that "Haven of Rest"...
Then God in His infinite wisdom
Will keep us Eternally blest.

Crescent Hill Baptist Church

TEST OF FAITH

It's easy to say we have "Faith" in God
    When everything goes our way,
It's easy to say "Thy Will Be Done"
    If we know we can somehow sway,
Out of the "Hands of our Master,"
    Into the hands of our own,
The things that we want and think we should have
    When already our needs are all known.
But the true and earnest Christian
    Will never attempt to sway,
Into his hands what he thinks he should have,
    Instead, he will accept and obey.

DeSoto Falls

"The Lord is my shepherd; I shall not want." Psalm 23:1

TRUTH

May the life that we live be devoted
To Him as we walk every day;
Filled completely with TRUTH and obedience,
Or else we will simply betray —
Both our Lord and the fact that our service
Means nothing in what we portray,
And we'll fail to possess our profession
Of TRUTH in a sorrowful way.

Tom Eller's Bible

WISDOM

The old preacher weakly
Walked to the pew,
So weak and so humble,
Only noticed by few;
His steps rather slow —
His eyes sort of dim,
With his Bible well worn
From his reading within.

The young preacher followed,
Stepping with zeal,
So eager and willing
With much zest to fulfill;
His words well chosen
From books he had read,
With new thoughts and ideas,
His people well fed.

Out in the church there was
Someone from week after week,
Just quietly observing,
With tears on the cheek;
The aged and the youth!
The wisdom – the zest,
Truth and philosophy –
It was almost a test.

That soul oft' grew weary
And yet deep within,
Pure peacefulness glowed —
There was no darkness of sin;
'Cause rightly dividing
The word and the truth,
Comes simply from gospel –
Not old age or youth!

SECTION IV

ENCOURAGEMENT, PRAYER, PEACE

Anna Ruby Falls

Deuteronomy 3:28   "But charge Joshua, and encourage him, and strengthen him: for he shall go over before this people, and he shall cause them to inherit the land which thou shalt see."

PSALM 100

Oh, make a joyful noise
Unto the Lord, ye lands;
And serve the Lord with great gladness,
While singing in a band.

Know that the Lord is God,
He hath made us serene;
We are His people, not ourselves,
The sheep of pastures green.

Enter into His gates
With praise and thankfulness;
Enter His courts with praise to Him,
Oh, bless His Holiness.

The Lord our God is good,
With mercy that shall last;
His truth will endure evermore,
Through generations past.

Old Barn near Lynch Mountain

PRAISE AND THANKSGIVING

Let us now forget life's cares
And life's heartaches everywhere;
Let's just pause in thankfulness,
For each day of blessedness.

Morning dew so fresh and clean,
Sparkling as the sunshine beams;
Gentle breezes flowing free,
Whispering through the lovely trees.

Flower petals opened wide
With a butterfly beside;
Graceful birds up in the sky,
Silently just passing by.

Streams that sing a rushing song
As their waters flow along;
Little stones with fresh, green moss,
Dandelions that sway and toss.

Children playing happily,
As if a care could never be;
Homes with doors that open wide
For strangers just to step inside.

Bright, full moons and ocean tides,
Golden fields of grain so wide;
A land where freedom ever rings
As voices blend and softly sing.

Praises to our God above,
Who has blessed us with His love;
May we then, from shore to shore,
Praise His name forevermore!

MOLD US

Our Potter in Heaven,
May we ask this of Thee?
To take us and beat us,
Tis our simple plea.

Just beat us, dear Potter,
Into workable clay;
Enabling Thy wisdom
To mold us Thy way.

That we could be vessels,
Holding "water of life";
Not broken cisterns which
Have cracked with much strife.

But vessels, Oh Potter,
Holding water divine;
From the "Fountain of Life,"
It's the purest we find.

Oh Potter in Heaven!
May we never complain!
Just take us and beat us
Even if there is pain!

Oh mold us, dear Potter,
For Thy Kingdom above;
And help us to serve Thee
With an undying love.

ENCOURAGEMENT

Several years ago an old sister
Took our hands and as she held them
She warmly said,
"Someday you'll understand it all,
For the word of God is like a puzzle,
And it fits together piece by piece."

Now we can relate to her wisdom,
For God's time has somewhat revealed
This piece by piece.
The puzzle is not completed,
But enough pieces are together
And it's forming a beautiful scene.

So let's continue to be patient.
A picturesque puzzle takes time
To complete it.
And as God reveals piece by piece,
Let's be willing to kindly pick them up,
To form an Eternal Scene.

Grace Calvary Episcopal Church, Clarkesville, GA

BLESSED MOMENTS

Ah, the bliss we have each Sunday
As we sit within the pews;
Gaining strength from the Good Shepherd,
While His path, we each pursue.

There our thirst is quenched with water,
While our hungry souls are fed;
There we feast on Heavenly manna
From the Gospels' broken bread.

There we find sweet satisfaction,
There we find rest and repose;
While God's flock is all together,
Sheltered from all of His foes.

Ah, the bliss we have each Sunday,
Precious, Quiet, Promised Peace;
Hopeful Joys, Anticipations —
May these moments never cease!

Old German Baptist Church, Cleveland, GA

HOLD FAST

If you seem to be low with the burdens of life
And you're tired of the long, dreary way;
You had better remember adversities come
So continue to constantly pray.

Be it sickness or sorrow or sadness or grief
That has broken your heart right in two;
Remember your Master has felt the same pain
And experienced the aches that you do.

So hold fast to your faith with a grip that is strong
And lean on your Master's right arm;
Then regardless what comes, if you're steadfast and true,
You'll be safe from all danger and harm.

Quince

AN EVENING PRAYER

My day's not completed, unless it's with God,
Forgiving my footsteps wherever I do trod;
So often they slip, and my feet go astray,
On into a path that may lead the wrong way.

Perhaps I just stumble, or drift to the side
On into a road that's a little too wide;
Before I retire then, my soul, for the night,
My prayers ascend, "Lord, please help me do right."

"I know I am weak, and my feet go astray,
My light seems to flicker along life's pathway;
My thoughts are so selfish, just centered on me,
I often forget to sing praises of Thee!"

"So often I want just whatever I ask,
Complaining if ever, I must do a task;
Dear Lord up in Heaven, please help me do right,
And keep me forever, held close in Thy sight!"

"Abide with me, Saviour, the day swiftly went,
The evening is here and my day is far spent;
Forgive me, and keep me throughout the long night,
Until I awaken to marvelous light!"

*"Evening, and morning, and at noon, will I pray, and cry aloud:
and he shall hear my voice."   Psalm 55:17*

IT'S SO SIMPLE

If we didn't love our Saviour,
If we didn't love our God,
If we didn't love His footsteps
Or the path that He has trod —
We'd fail, we'd fall, we'd tremble,
We wouldn't know the way,
That God has simply taught us
To walk from day to day.

So simple, oh so simple!
In words of black and white;
Just read, then yield with duty,
So simple and so right!
God's love has made it easy,
Yet we tend to complicate
Commands that are so simple —
We even violate.

Perhaps, sometimes we shudder
When we pause to realize,
How we complicate simplicity
As we tend to compromise.
But think of Christ in Heaven,
He no doubt shudders too,
With pain that pierces like the sword
That He once felt and knew.

So if we love our Saviour,
And if we love our God,
And if we love His footsteps,
We'll love the path He trod.
We'll love His truth so simple,
We'll yield to His commands,
We'll want to serve him better —
Let's simply understand!

SOMEDAY IT'LL ALL BE OVER

Someday it'll all be over,
All this turmoil, hate and strife;
Someday it'll all be over
We'll enter a better life.

All sorrows gone forever,
No disappointments to face;
Someday it'll all be over,
We'll win the glorious race!

Someday it'll all be over,
Discouraged moments will flee;
We'll reign forever in Heaven —
A place for you and me.

Someday it'll all be over,
All worries and cares will cease;
We'll live in Heaven with Jesus,
A Kingdom of love and peace!

Someday it'll all be over,
Sickness and heartaches no more;
Someday it'll all be over,
We'll meet on the golden shore!

So if you get discouraged
And feel the load's too rough;
Keep going and never falter,
There's nothing that's too tough.

Someday it'll all be over,
All this turmoil, hate and strife;
Someday it'll all be over.
We'll enjoy a better life.

A PRAYER

My way is dark and sometimes drear,
I fear I'll go astray;
Temptations knock and knock again,
Oh help me Lord, I pray.

I fear somewhere along the way
I'll yield to Satan's call –
It won't be much – I know it won't,
But Lord, I still might fall.

You see, the devil has a way
Of carrying out deceit;
And Lord, I fear, I really fear,
That's where I'll meet defeat.

He's here - so close to all of us,
At home, at church – he's there!
His cunning ways – so crafty, Lord,
He's almost everywhere!

He's ebbed his way in sermons Lord,
He's even in some songs;
Deceitful music with a beat,
And Lord, I know it's wrong!

He's prepared us packaged sermons,
For convenience – one stop deals;
He's mixed in lots of fables
Just to give the heart a thrill.

Oh Lord, how much, I ask how much
Of this can I endure?
Help me dear Lord, just help me Lord,
To be firm and staunch and sure!

CLOSER DRAWN TO THEE

Oh Father, draw us close to Thee
And keep us in Thy sight;
Closer, Oh closer drawn to Thee,
Engulfed in Thy delight.

Oh draw us closer, still we pray,
And let us rest in Thee;
In total comfort, total love,
So boundless, rich and free.

Oh closer, closer, let us flee,
Where we can warmly share;
Thy tender mercy and Thy love
Surrounded everywhere!

Oh draw us closer, closer Lord,
Protect us from all harm;
Keep holding us secure and safe
In Thy dear precious arms.

Oh Father, draw us closer yet,
Remind us of Thy will;
Closer and closer drawn to Thee,
Lord, even closer still.

TIDES OF PREPARATION

When all of life's tides run against you,
And your spirit is downcast and low;
Remember there's One up in Heaven
Who is ready and willing to show,
That life and its labors are weighty
With disappointed heartaches and cares,
You have but to tell Him your troubles,
For He's ready and waiting to share.
He will lift your spirit up higher
Than the wings of a swift, soaring bird,
But first, you must trust in your Master,
And believe in His Own written Word.
He knows when to send little burdens
Which will help keep you humble and small,
While your spirit and soul keep on thriving
And growing in heights that are tall.
So pause and relax when life's burdens
Appear heavy, and just understand –
It's only your Master in Heaven
Preparing your soul for His land.

Sutton Mill, Clarkesville, GA

CROSSES INSTEAD OF CROWNS

Lord, give us a cross
Instead of a crown;
For in so doing,
There's much to be found.
Crosses are heavy,
The crowns are so light,
But crosses we find
Are a pure delight!

For each precious cross
That falls on our way;
Just makes us realize
We need God each day.
We find crosses leave
Some wounds and much pain,
Reminding us often
That our Christ was slain.

We find that a cross
Teaches humbleness too,
Meekness and Temperance,
In all that we do.
Longsuffering, Gentleness,
Peace, Joy and Love;
Goodness and Faith —
So much from above!

Lord, send us a cross
Instead of a crown;
Teach us pure wisdom
That's steadfast and sound.
Wisdom to know that
Each cross from above;
Is sent by our Master
With Kindness and Love!

NEVER GIVE UP

Don't ever give up when the road gets rough
And all hope has vanished away;
For if life is dark and full of despair,
Hope on for a brighter day!
Now hope may grow dim but never give up,
Regardless whatever our lot;
For hope is something we all must possess
When the battles of life are fought.

Hope keeps us alive when the battles of life,
Look like they can never be won;
Hope conquers despair, rejection and fear,
When we say "Thy will be done."
For then, when we've won the battle we fought,
And hope is reality now;
We're guaranteed winners – no matter what,
When we hope, submit and allow.

**Tree along path to
Anna Ruby Falls**

ROMANTIC FRIENDSHIP

As the ebbing morning light breaks thru,
Flickering rays, unblemished and new—
I think of you!

As the countless millions labor long,
Into mid-morning with sweat and song—
I think of you!

As the peak of noon swiftly appears,
With brilliant beams of sunlight to share—
I think of you!

As the evening rays quietly fade
Into beautiful golden shades—
I think of you!

Into a friendship reverently,
Sealed with a bond of fraternity—
Eternally.

Bill and Kaye Bryan's Home

INSTRUMENTS

Our lives are like an instrument
Of many, many strings,
If played each day in beauty,
The melody will ring.

Two strings are simple little hands,
Two strings are just our feet,
Two strings, our eyes, two strings, our ears,
Our tongue, a string so sweet.

We then must pull each special string
To blend sweet melody,
Never too hard, never too soft,
With care pull easily.

And if we pull the strings wisely
As we walk from day to day,
We'll find the melody to be
Joyful along the way.

We'll find our God in Heaven
Will enjoy this music too
For our lives are merely instruments
In everything we do.

*"Sing unto the LORD with the harp; with the harp,
and the voice of a psalm."*   *Psalm 98:5*

DAILY MUSIC

Listen to the daily music
Which starts early in the day;
Chirping birds by countless species
Seem to sing their hearts away.

Yet we mortals often grumble
And complain with deep despair;
Doubts and fears o'er take our moments,
Concerning groans are everywhere.

Can't we daily sing our praises
Like the common little birds?
Sending echoes to their Master,
Unaware of being heard?

Oh let's send our praises upward
To our Master's throne on high;
Like the thousand, countless species,
Singing praises thru the skies.

"Make a joyful noise unto the LORD, all ye lands." Psalm 100:1

COUNT YOUR BLESSINGS

Let's count our many blessings,
When life seems dark and blue;
Count them all, don't miss a one,
And we will see it's true,
That our troubles are outnumbered
By the blessings we receive,
But until we count them one by one ---
It's no use for us to believe,
That our Father up in Heaven
Sends such blessings down below,
As He scatters them upon us
So richly to and fro.

Our troubles then become so small
That we almost feel ashamed,
That we let such little simple trials
Create such terrible pain.
So when we get downcast
And feel as though we've met,
Life's darkest moment, darkest night,
Let's start counting and forget,
The burdens that confront us
As we walk along the way,
And count our many blessings
That our Father sends each day.

**Sutton Mill,
Clarkesville, GA**

REMEMBER THY CREATOR

Remember thy Creator
In the days of thy youth,
For there's nothing to lose
But to gain, there is truth.
For what can a man give
In exchange for his soul—
Not even the whole world
Could pay for his toll,
To enter the gate
Into Heaven above,
Where surrounding the throne
Is peace, joy and love.
So why not start out
Early in life,
Even though we must meet
Trials, burdens and strife.
There's a crown waiting for us
And our toll isn't high,
But of course we must pay
For the burdens by and by.
And that isn't hard
When God earnestly cares,
As He gently eases
All of our fears.
So why not start out,
Early in youth
Sell all that you have,
Buy nothing but truth.

PSALM 23

"The LORD is my shepherd; I shall not want.

He maketh me to lie down in green pastures: he leadeth me beside the still waters.

He restoreth my soul: he leadeth me in the paths of righteousness for his name's sake.

Yea, though I walk through the valley of the shadow of death, I will fear no evil: for thou art with me; thy rod and thy staff they comfort me.

Thou preparest a table before me in the presence of mine enemies: thou anointest my head with oil; my cup runneth over.

Surely goodness and mercy shall follow me all the days of my life: and I will dwell in the house of the LORD for ever."

SECTION V

DEATH

Skylake

Rev. 20:12 "And I saw the dead, small and great, stand before God; and the books were opened: which is the book of life; and the dead were judged out of those things which were written in the books, according to their works."

DEATH IS BUT A FLOWER

At the close of each day
God holds in His Hands,
A bouquet of flowers...
Which He picked through the lands.

Sometimes they are little
Just starting to bloom,
And we wonder just why . . .
They must go to the tomb.

Sometimes they're in blossom,
So happy and bright,
And we wonder just why . . .
They must drift out of sight.

Sometimes they are older,
Their petals all worn,
And we wonder just why. . .
They can't live on.

At the close of this world
In the Heavens above,
Just think of the flowers...
In vases of Love.

Bill and Kaye Bryan's Home

LETTER FROM HEAVEN

Dear Daddy and Mommy—

Just thought I'd write a little note
To thank you for my care;
Your love and kindness seemed to be
Much more than just my share.
I longed to hug your shoulders that
Had bore the weight of me;
I longed to crawl and play with toys
So swift and easily.

But I was just an angel sent,
Appearing in disguise;
My little form was certainly
Not pleasant to the eyes.
My life was not the easiest,
I had to struggle too;
I'll not forget my last dear day
I had to spend with you.

It seemed I climbed a tall ladder
With all my strength and might;
And when, at last, I reached the top,
I took my angel flight.
And then it seemed you had to blink,
For you to see how clear
The crystal streets of Heaven were —
Oh! Won't you join me there?

Keep climbing up the ladder rungs,
Faint not with load and care;
Climb on, with all your strength and might,
I'm waiting for you here!
Where we can walk the crystal streets
And praise our Master's skill,
Who formed my frame out of the dust,
According to His will.

Love,

Your Special Child

*"Suffer little children to come unto me, and forbid them not:
for of such is the kingdom of God."*   *St. Luke 18:16*

THE LAST BOUQUET

The air was crisp, the sky was clear,
While we strolled down the lane;
Gathering flowers for the last bouquet—
E'er spring should come again.

Many a blossom flourished gay,
The colors vast and bright;
Gave many hours and gave many days,
A picture of delight.

Our thoughts went to the last bouquet,
That God someday will pick;
Gathering souls for His kingdom above,
When time no longer ticks.

Oh, that our souls with petals bright,
Will flourish on that day;
Without any droop or even a fade—
Picked for the last bouquet.

Bill and Kaye Bryan's Home

SECTION VI

NATURE

Anna Ruby Falls

2 Peter 1:4 "Whereby are given unto us exceeding great and precious promises: that by these ye might be partakers of the divine nature, having escaped the corruption that is in the world through lust."

AN ARTIST

"The earth is the Lord's
And the fulness thereof,"
And we've certainly been blessed
With an Artist from above.
His strokes are so graceful,
While His brush moves with ease,
As He paints the earth's face
To the top of the trees.
Then He colors the fields
A dark golden brown,
And with the stroke of His brush
Corn shocks can be found.
Along with some pumpkins
To help brighten the fields
And fill up our fruit shelves—
A harvest to yield!
Then He mixes more paint
To color the sky

A deep brilliant blue with
Clouds of lace to pass by.
And with the stroke of His brush,
He makes the connection
Between sky and the clouds
To give water, reflection.
Then leaving enough rays
Of light to shine through,
He brings out the highlights
With various colors of hues.
Indeed, we've been blessed
With an Artist from above,
"The earth is the Lord's
And the fulness thereof."

BEAUTIFUL VALLEYS

There are beautiful valleys
While walking within
And the lessons we find
Are taught only by Him,
For the mountain-top moments
Are blessings indeed,
But the beautiful valleys,
Germinate fertile seeds.

There are beautiful valleys
With shadows and shade,
But nothing's too dark
That the Son our God made.
Though the mountain-top moments
Are sometimes disguised,
All the beautiful valleys
Should not be despised.

There are beautiful valleys
Filled with fountains that flow,
Which teach us great lessons
That God wants us to know.
There's rest for the weary
Near the pools, deep within,
Ah! The beautiful valleys
Given only by Him.

Pasture at Smithgall

EROSION

Last night we took a little walk
 Along a country road,
And to our right we viewed a field
That had not yet been sown.

The field had just been plowed and there
Were furrows deep and wide,
Erosion seemed to take its toll,
A fact that one can't hide.

We couldn't help but further think
How souls could do the same,
Erode with furrows deep and wide
And oft there is a blame.

Sometimes we can't control the cause,
But we MUST do our BEST,
To stop erosion of the soul
And God will do the rest.

Psalms 129:3 "*The plowers plowed upon my back: they made long their furrows.*"

HARVEST ANSWER

Standing under the old oak tree
The Father and Son stood still,
Another day of hard work done,
Thankfully they looked over the hill.
"Father, I've got a question,
If you'll notice the fields that are gold,
Some stems are tall, some stems are short,"
And this is what he was told.

"Well, Son, take a look at you and me,
You stand so sturdy and strong,
While my back is bent with the burdens of life
I've carried on my shoulders so long.
Your hair, so handsome-like, waves through the wind,
Like the wheat that is tall and in bloom,
And mine, see how gray, the "Harvest" is near –
I'm stepping toward my tomb.

But soon, dear son, my place you'll take,
And your back, like the wheat, will bend,
And then you will tell to your son, who is tall,
Of the "Harvest" to come again."

Circle C Ranch

CLEANSING DEW

Just as the dew gently cleanses the earth
As each day is reborn thru the dawn,
 Totally spotless, refreshed and anew,
From the mountains to gardens and lawn.

Thoroughly cleansed from all yesterday's filth,
 Dreadful dirt, dreadful dust, dreadful stain;
Forgotten at last! Remembered no more,
Of all blemish and possible pain.

Similar thus, do we find that our souls
Can be spotless, reborn and kept new;
By the cleansing blood that our Saviour shed,
Like the earth, He's our soul cleansing dew.

But we must confess all guilt and all filth,
 And we'll find He most kindly forgives;
Freedom at last! Remembered no more!
What a life of refreshment to live!

Sutton Mill, Clarkesville, GA

ETERNAL BEAUTY

There are places God's created
Where we stand in total awe;
As His handiwork surrounds us,
Endless beauty seems no flaw.

Ah! The lushness of the forest,
Crisp and green, so pure and clear;
One could pause and rest forever
In the cool, calm atmosphere.

While the water trickles slowly
From the lofty mountain heights;
Down into a peaceful valley,
Oh, the beauty of such sights!

But awaiting up in Heaven
Is a place that far exceeds;
Human eyes and earthly beauty,
For this earth just supersedes.

The tree of life—Eternity—
'Midst the streams that will not dry;
Fountains free near the paths serene,
This awaits us in the sky.

It's impossible to fathom
All His mighty, grand design;
Though when beckoned by earth's beauty,
This is just a taste we find.

GREAT VOYAGE

Our lives are like a great voyage,
Upon the ocean's sea;
We cannot choose the weather that
God sends to you and me.

Oft times the storms of sorrows fall,
While we forget to view;
Beyond the clouds, so thick, so dark—
A light is beaming through.

Not 'til the ship has landed safe
On Heaven's golden shore;
Will God unveil the thunderheads,
Which seemed so dark before.

Explaining carefully the need
Of FAITH on storm tossed seas;
Accompanied with angelic host
To live Eternally.

Mallard Duck

SOMEWHERE

Somewhere in the fiercest storm
We find the winds are calm;
Somewhere on the painful bed
We find a healing balm.

Somewhere in the darkest night
We find a candle glows;
Somewhere in a rushing stream
We find it smoothly flows.

Somewhere in the blackest cloud
We find a silver line;
Somewhere in our busy lives
We find some unused time.

Somewhere all our grief and woes
Will gently pass away;
Oh the joys that burn within,
If we could somehow say...

Somewhere there's a stepping stone,
Toward our Eternal goal;
Where we will reign forever,
He cares for our dear souls!

"And he arose, and rebuked the wind, and said unto the sea,
Peace, be still. And the wind ceased, and there was a great calm."
St. Mark 4:39

THE VINE

As we cling to the Vine
May the branches we find,
Be strong and healthy within;
For truly we know
That nothing will grow,
Unless we abide in HIM.

As we cling to the Vine
May the branches we find,
Be purged and pruned within;
For branches can wind
And fruitless entwine,
Unless we abide in HIM.

As we cling to the Vine
May the branches we find,
Bear fruit again and again;
For fruit will not yield,
Abundant in fields,
Unless we abide in HIM.

As we cling to the Vine
May the branches we find,
Bear peace, joy and love within;
For truly we find
Fruit clings to a vine,
And that Vine alone — is HIM.

BLUEBIRD

I heard a blue bird softly sing
In tones that were so sweet,
I paused and listened carefully,
It was a joyous treat.
For the song was full assurance,
Sent by our God above,
That all our friends and family
Are protected by His love.

So if distance seems a problem
And miles seem far away,
Just listen to the bluebird
As it sings from day to day.
For it's God's way of reminding
And assuring all is well,
By just a simple bluebird
That sings so sweet and swell.

Sutton Mill, Clarkesville, GA

GOLDEN GARDEN DEEDS

It's time to till the soil
And plant the little seeds,
Hoping to have a "Harvest,"
Yielding golden deeds.

A row of Peas we'll start with,
Carefully sowing by hand,
*P*atience, *P*erseverance and *P*rayer,
We'll try planting throughout the land.

Next a little Lettuce
We'll drop along the way,
Let us be helpful and understanding,
And *Let us* continue to pray.

Next a row or two of Squash,
This too, we'll carefully sow,
Squash prejudice and jealousy
And the gossip too often we know.

Last of all some Turnips,
For "Harvest" in the fall,
Turn up for Sunday Meetings,
And *Turn up* with love for all.

SALT

The other day we took some salt
And placed it on some meat,
Then closed the lid and just sat back
Upon our rocking seat.
The simple salt did several things,
Upon that piece of meat,
And in the end — that piece of meat
Gave us a special treat.
Salt changes things without a noise,
The impact is so great,
Salt flavors things down in the pores
And deeply penetrates.
Salt also heals and soothes the wounds
That hurts and aches and smarts;
Salt's just a simple little grain,
But needed for our hearts.

"Ye are the salt," our Saviour said,
This impact should be great,
The noise we make should not be heard –
It should just penetrate.
We should encourage those around
With happy attitudes,
The flavors that we leave behind
Should be of gratitude.
Our thoughts of others should be kind,
Caring and sharing too,
An understanding heart will lift
And soothe the soul that's blue.
"Ye are the salt," our Saviour said,
Use it upon your meat;
And in the end — that piece of meat,
Will bring Eternal treats.

LOWERING THE SUNSET

Another day is finished!
Another day is done!
And God is gently lowering
The golden evening sun;
Hanging out the canopy
Filled with stars so bright,
To guide the weary pilgrim
As he struggles through the night.
For each little star is a peep hole
To Heaven's beautiful street,
And the pilgrim is always ready
To close his day and meet,
God's encouragement for him to continue
The Journey in which he begun,
Reminding him soon he'll be finished
And the VICTORY at last will be won.

WHITER THAN SNOW

The ground outside is covered softly
With a blanket of white snow,
And, oh, what beauty sent from Heaven
To cover the earth's face below.

It's when we see such beauty,
That our thoughts begin to flow,
How we wish our souls were whiter
Than the blanket God sent to glow.

But soon the snow gets dirty
As it disappears and melts,
And our sins are just as noticeable,
While our soul, so weak is felt.

But the encouragement that's given
When we see the ground so white,
Gives us strength to continue the struggle,
And never give up the fight.

FROST OR FRUIT

Once an old man with an orchard of fruit,
Stood viewing and counting his crop,
Satisfied he did seem,
As he quietly beamed,
With hope of a record to top.

But God's power and infinite wisdom,
Turned the dew drops into a frost,
Broken hearted he was,
And all simply because,
His orchard of fruit was a loss.

Frustrated he was – about to give up –
His vigor – decayed and all lost,
He said, "How could my God,
Freeze the dew, trees and sod,
And kill all my fruit with a frost?

Then a kind hearted friend came passing by,
And gave him a listening ear,
He encouraged with love,
As he focused above,
On the fruit that God's children bear.

The man slowly turned and bowed down his head,
Ashamed of his action and thought,
'Cause fruit of the Spirit,
Is greater in merit,
Than his orchard that came to naught.

II Kings 13:17:
  "And he said, Open the window eastward. And he opened it ....."

SECTION VII

CHRISTMAS

Bill and Kaye Bryan's Home

Luke 2:13-14 "*And suddenly there was with the angel a multitude of the heavenly host praising God, and saying, Glory to God in the highest, and on earth peace, good will toward men.*"

THE INN

Inn a stable, *inn* a manger, *inn* the starlight,
Once He laid,
Calm and Peaceful, simply lovely,
Without blemish,
Was the Babe.

He was born for us a Saviour, and a prophet,
Priest and King,
He was born for our redemption –
He was born, oh
Let us sing.

What a blessing, what a promise, what a special
Joy Divine,
Just to know Him, just to love Him,
Just to praise Him
By mankind.

Oh how gentle, oh how lovely, oh how blessed,
Is our Gift,
Let us hold Him, keep Him near us,
Listen to Him,
While we lift...

Our Hosannas, ever upward, ever praising
All the time,
Till in glory, we behold HIM –
Then forever,
Sweet sublime.

NO ROOM

No room! No room in Bethlehem!
No room! No room in the Inn!
Yes, room for affluent, riches and wealth,
But no room for the poor to come in.

How sad! How sad we cry aloud,
How sad! No room in the Inn!
How could we leave our Master outside
To be born of a virgin within?

On down the ages we've traveled,
Down to this moment of time,
Is there room for our precious Master
To be kept in our hearts all sublime?

Yes room! Yes room for our Saviour!
Yes room! Yes room in the "Inn;"
Oh let's all remain true and faithful,
Keeping "room" for Him unto the end.

Luke 2:7 *"And she brought forth her firstborn son, and wrapped him in swaddling clothes, and laid him in a manger; because there was no room for them in the inn."*

SECTION VIII

GOLDEN GEMS

Eller Home

Revelation 21:18 "And the building of the wall of it was *of* jasper: and the city *was* pure gold, like unto clear glass."

WHAT IS A FRIEND?

What is a friend? A friend is a person whom you highly respect and one whom you are willing to take advice from, whether you agree or not. It is someone that is always ready to listen to a broken voice and try to comfort the deepest trouble within one's breast. There are just as many different kinds of friends as there are different types of stars in the sky above. There are friends that seem to flicker and almost fade away, but yet, there is some little spark that keeps them glittering. There are friends that are inspiring and seem to always be sending the same amount of rays of light into the vast unknown — not too bright and not too dim. There are friends that always seem so happy and gay, burning all their ambition into the brightest beam ever seen, until suddenly, without warning, there is only a dim cast left blazing, waiting for an opportunity to pick up strength again. Who is your friend? Is it someone that flickers dimly? Is it someone that is inspiring? Is it someone who is full of ambition? A friend is someone that can enjoy the many different kinds of people just like the many different types of stars that God so carefully placed in the sky above. A friend doesn't just like one, or two, but a real friend cares for all.

LIFE

Life isn't always like a lovely rose, standing in a beautiful long necked vase upon the table in the corner of your room. It isn't always as graceful and as charming as the picture painted by an author of an interesting fable or story of love. Life is made up of many hardships resting upon the shoulders of every individual. Some people only seem to have a few heartaches through life while others are burdened every minute with tears flowing down their warm cheeks, dropping upon their troubled breast and leaving stains of melted warmth. Sometimes it is because a loved one has been picked to fill a vase in the Heavens above. Sometimes it is because little boys and girls are seeking for parents, only to find themselves as little orphans in this large world of ours. Sometimes it is because of a handicap that many people seem to suffer from pain or laughs and sneers made by people who do not comprehend how thankful they really should be. Sometimes it is even from a deep scar left upon the heart of a young girl or boy who has fallen in love and for some reason – could not forget. Indeed, life isn't all roses and if you will notice the tree outside your window, you will see some scars on the bark, some of the limbs are missing and several knot holes are more prominent than others. And yet, if you will look deep into your own heart, you too will find many scars. However, you need to realize that each little scar and each little tear that falls, only helps to make you stronger to accept the hardships to come, just like the scars and knot holes in trees help strengthen them to be able to withstand stronger storms.

Go ahead!
    Flap your wings
        Like the gossamer butterfly
And gracefully sail
    Into your land of dreams.....

Keep sailing!
    On and on!
        For in so doing your array
Of grace and beauty
    Forms a dream of its own.

Just as the trees in the forest,
Lean on each other for strength,
We too, need those about us,
To fulfill all our days at length.

      For support is often needed
      From those who are oft close by,
      Lifting our inward spirits
      To heights that are higher than high.

Path to DeSoto Falls

Little seeds drifting
　　　Through the air
　　　　Quietly landing
In secret places
　　　To bring forth beauty of its own . . .

Reminds us how one
　　　Eagerly
　　　　Will drop deeds of kindness
In special ways
　　　To those in life, both young and old.

One of the greatest satisfactions
Ever obtained
Is quiet solitude, which yields
        Inner joy,
            Inner hope and
                Inner peace.

Such virtues cannot be destroyed
If the factor of time
Is allotted each day,
        By pausing
            And reflecting
                On these things.

Path to Anna Ruby Falls

Do not let death
Become a fear...
    For there's a time to weep,
    And a time to even mourn;
For those we love and cherish
And who walked with us each day.

SO

Be not afraid
To shed a tear ...
    For God Himself, sends drops
    Of rain upon the earth;
And in return, the flowers
Grow and frolic in the wind.

Eller Home

Now if, per chance,
You see a bird,
Go soaring through the sky,
It's only God,
Reminding you,
That special prayers fly:

From all your friends
And family
And those who really care
For prayers, thoughts
And lots of love,
Just come from everywhere!

True love will never die,
It grows and grows from
The tiniest bud,
And brightens in the sky

SO

May your life together...
Unfold each petal
Into a bloom,
Blossoming forever!

Today is special ....

It's time to pause and reflect over the past
And it's time to look forward to the future.
It's time for friends and family
To embrace you with love,
To acknowledge your presence,
And your very being.
It's time for those who care to just simply say ...
That this is your day and we want to share it
With you because we simply care
About you, you're special...
And special people deserve
Special days...
Like today.

May it help to bring you comfort
Just to know that others care,
Just to know your grieving moments
Are by others, being shared.
Just to know these parting moments,
Which just seem to tug and tear,
Will all vanish at the meeting
With our loved ones, over there!

If life didn't have sorrow,
Would we need the tomorrows?

Life must have sorrow,
For a better tomorrow,
Filled with Eternal joy,
Which seems to capture the soul!

There is a place
Where the Saints of all Ages
Will bask and frolic forever.

There...
    No more pain,
        Nor heartache,
            Nor sorrow,
All will be peace forevermore.

May the peace which passes all understanding,
    Be Yours.

DeSoto Falls

Below Anna Ruby Falls

Eternity –
  Oh, how it rings
    Louder and Clearer and Sweeter.

Echoing on and on
  Drawing us closer and closer
    As we yearn for it more and more.

Eternity –
  Oh, how it rings,
    May our souls ever rest
    In God's Eternity.

Silver hair and wrinkles
    Are no longer anything to be ashamed of.
It's God's way of gracefully preparing his own
    For a Golden Tomorrow.

Tomorrow,
Our lives will be over on this earth
    Only memories
        Be they good or bad
           Will be left.

Tomorrow,
We look forward to a Golden Tomorrow,
    Eternally
        With HIM!

Path to DeSoto Falls

Numbers 17:5 *"And it shall come to pass, that the man's rod, whom I shall choose, shall blossom: and I will make to cease from me the murmurings of the children of Israel, whereby they murmur against you."*

SECTION IX

MISCELLANEOUS

Lynch Mountain Barn

Ephesians 1:1-3 "*Paul, an apostle of Jesus Christ by the will of God, to the saints which are at Ephesus, and to the faithful in Christ Jesus: Grace be to you, and peace, from God our Father, and from the Lord Jesus Christ. Blessed be the God and Father of our Lord Jesus Christ, who hath blessed us with all spiritual blessings in heavenly places in Christ:*"

PAUL AND SILAS

If your life is filled with setbacks
And your days appear to be blue,
Keep singing like Paul and Silas
And the gates will open for you.

Sing on and sing on until midnight,
Keep singing right on thru the night,
And you'll find a gate will open
Where freedom at last, is in sight.

For problems are oft like prisons,
With iron bars that never will break;
But oh, if you'll just keep singing
The ground will eventually break.

The bars of iron will diminish
And the jailor will fall asleep,
If you just keep right on singing
Regardless what trials you may meet.

*"And at midnight Paul and Silas prayed, and sang praises
unto God: and the prisoners heard them."   Acts 16:25*

SUBTLENESS

The serpent was more subtle
Than any beast of the field,
Which the Lord God made
In His garden to yield.

Today there's no difference
Than what was ever before,
Subtleness creeping
Around slyly, but sure.

So beware lest the serpent
Somehow deceives you and I;
Sly with his manner
As he claims we won't die.

For the voice of our Lord God
Will surely call us someday,
Firmly, "Where art Thou?"
Then just what will we say?

Genesis 3:1   "Now the serpent was more subtil than any beast of the field which the LORD God had made. And he said unto the woman, Yea, hath God said, Ye shall not eat of every tree of the garden?"

HUMANITY

All around the global earth,
On land from shore to shore;
We find humanity exists,
Mass numbers, more and more.

Ah, me thinks and wonders too,
What's deep within each soul;
Who is their God? How do they live?
And just what are their goals?

Some seem so cold and brutish,
While others seem quite warm;
And yet each has a soul within,
With bodies that God formed.

Oh, that each soul upon the earth,
Would strive to do its best;
And grow into a lasting soul,
That'll pass the Master's test.

*Psalms 1:6   "For the LORD knoweth the way of the righteous:
but the way of the ungodly shall perish."*

THE TEST

Will we hold out unto the end,
When tried and tried some more?
Will we be firm? Will we be bold,
As those who went before?

The time has come and we must face
Adversities again,
Economies are failing fast,
Projecting mighty men...

Who're seeking for the answers
To the problems that we face,
Affecting every creed of man
Within the human race.

It's nothing new to those who know
The Bible and the word,
Our God's revealing prophecy,
For He is Lord of Lords.

Let come what may and let's not fear
What seems to be ahead;
"Be faithful to the utmost end,"
This -- God himself has said.

WILD OATS

Wild oats had been my motto,
And I sowed an acre or two;
But when I finally started to harvest,
I found the grains were few.

The chaff came by the bushel,
The straw was tall and thin,
I wondered where the grains were,
So empty was my bin.

So I turned to my book of records,
And there in letters of red –
I read why my loss was greater,
And this is what it said...

"Some have fallen by the wayside,
Some fell on stony ground,
Still others fell among the thorns,
Choking them – not to be found.

But he that sowed the good seed
Is the Son of God;
Your harvest will be greater,
Sixty fold will come from your sod."

You see, my records didn't balance,
My harvest was almost a loss;
But I hope that someone can profit
From this lesson at my cost.

TOWERS OF POWER

The towers of power are forceful today,
Men build to their highest esteem;
It's like long ago, in a country well known,
The "Tower of Babel" was seen.

Seems the higher one climbs, the greater we are,
Men like to be viewed by all;
Such towers of power will crumble away,
Beware! Lest there'll be a great fall.

There are powers that tower — great is the force,
Along with foundations secure;
Confusion and strife isn't found anywhere,
Where powers that tower are pure.

Oh, that our towers are of the right power
As we build obediently;
When directed by God — our towers won't fall,
As they climb to eternity.

*"So the LORD scattered them abroad from thence
upon the face of all the earth" Genesis 11:8*

TERMITES

There are termites in the Temple
Of the living Church of God,
And they're breaking down the pillars
With their subtle little gnaws.
They're gnawing here and gnawing there,
Gnawing where they should not gnaw,
And soon the pillars stand no more,
As they crumble down and fall.

There are termites in the Temple
Of the living Church of God,
And they're drilling holes with power,
Forming dusty, spongy sod.
It is weakening the pillars,
In the spongy sod they sink,
And soon the pillars stand no more,
While the termites laugh and wink.

Oh, exterminate the termites
With thy powerful sword and shield,
Spray from the written word of God
And no longer let them yield.
Oh, exterminate the termites,
For they gnaw with power and force,
The Temple of our living God —
Oh, it's time to reinforce.

Let's exterminate the Temple
Of the living Church of God,
With spiritual insecticides,
Deep into the sod;
Throughout the living Church of God,
Which should pure and spotless be,
Upheld by pillars of the truth,
Which will last Eternally.

WATCH OUT

When things go well
And our life seems swell,
And our burdens appear to be light,
When we joyously sing,
With echoes that ring,
Perhaps it's time to WATCH OUT.

When nothing goes wrong,
And our voice is a song,
And our labors just seem to go right,
Tho' relaxed for a while,
Pacified with a smile,
Perhaps it's time to WATCH OUT.

When we have won
A victory well done,
In battles we're given to fight,
When even we've reached
Our mountain top peak,
Perhaps it's time to WATCH OUT.

For nothing we find,
Ever proven with time,
Will give Satan a better delight,
Then seeing our souls,
Quite content with our goals,
Perhaps it's time to WATCH OUT.

WHAT IF ?

"What If" is a question which often prevails,
With all the uncertainties of life.
"What If" and What If" – oh, how it grows,
While our doubts surmount to great strife.

But "What If" our Master would never have shared
With mankind, His salvation's great plan?
"What If" He kept His strength to Himself,
And cared not for one mortal man?

And "What If" His plan of redemption He kept
All alone in the Heavens above?
And "What If" He kept all to Himself,
His wisdom - His kindness - His love.

"What If" the sparrow and the grain of the field,
Were not watered and fed by God's care?
And "What If" our hands never could touch
The hem of the garment He wears?

So when the "What Ifs" surmount in our lives,
While the doubts and fears tend to prevail,
"If What" He assures — we can accept,
Our "What Ifs" will certainly fail.

"Trust in the LORD, and do good; so shalt thou dwell in the land,
and verily thou shalt be fed."   *Psalm 37:3*

RUMORS

Did you ever hear a rumor
And you thought that it was true,
And you passed it to another
Adding something to it new?

Just a little word you added
Thinking it wouldn't cause much harm,
And the next person did the same,
Thinking this won't cause alarm.

So the little rumor travels
From another day by day,
Growing larger as it passes...
What did you receive in pay?

Maybe you thought it a pleasure,
Adding just a little line,
Remember somehow, somebody
Will just have to pay the fine.

The next time you hear a rumor,
STOP! Don't spread it anymore,
It's going to hurt somebody,
Simply throw it out the door.

SET YOUR HOUSE IN ORDER

Set your house in order
Before you go to bed,
Who knows, you might get company
Before the sun turns red.

So keep your Bibles open,
Fill up your lamps with oil,
Who knows, it might be Jesus,
Your precious King so Royal.

So clean the dirt and cobwebs,
Polish up the rust,
Then throw away the musty rag
That's full of all the dust.

You see, the dirt and cobwebs,
Equals the filth of your mind,
The rusted grooves and edges,
Hold grudges from time to time.

So set your house in order
And gather up the dust,
You know it's always harder
When something starts to rust.

Sutton Mill
Clarkesville, GA

TELLING ON YOURSELF

You tell on yourself
By the friends that you seek,
By the topics in which you desire to speak.
You tell on yourself
By the clothes that you wear,
By the way that you act or the way that you care.
You tell on yourself
By the way that you talk,
The way that you laugh and the way that you walk.
You tell on yourself
By the way that you share,
With others the burdens that are heavy to bear.

Barrett Farm

You tell on yourself
How you employ your time,
By the way you make use of your spare dollars and dimes.
You tell on yourself
By the books that you choose,
From the well filled shelves that are yours to use.
You tell on yourself
By all of these ways,
And so many more too numerous to say.
So there's really no reason
And really no sense,
To try to put on a false pretense.

GOD ISN'T DEAD

So many are trying to tell us
That God has been dead for years;
But too many things in this world
Only show that God really cares.
Our God isn't dead – He's still living!
'Cause each morning we open our eyes,
We see the sunshine sparkle
Through the dew for miles and miles.

We hear the birds gently singing,
Sending melody into the air,
We hear a far away rumble
Of water flowing somewhere.
We see the fields of golden wheat,
We see the orchards of trees,
Now try to tell us God is dead ---
After all these things you see.
Well, man can't send the sunshine,
And man can't make the dew,
Never yet have we heard of a man
Gently chirping a song – have you?

No, and man can't color the golden fields
So richly blessed with grain,
Neither can man truthfully say,
An apple grows without rain.
Now how can anyone ever say
Those horrible words — "God's dead?"
We're afraid someday those people
Will face something we won't have to dread.

MOMENTS OF VALUE

Life has a special purpose,
We each have a job to do,
Too often we catch ourselves loafing,
Could this be said of you?

Each day we have many moments
Of spare time on our hands,
Just think of the many minutes
That are wasted through our lands.
If we'd just drop a golden deed
Somewhere along the way,
Words of kindness or a smile
Could brighten someone's day.
If we'd visit the sick and afflicted,
Lying in hospital beds;
Words of comfort are always welcome
To those with loved ones dead,
If we'd visit the widows and orphans,
Encouragement they need too,
Their pathway has been rugged,
Lonely, tiring and blue.
If our hearts were filled with Thanksgiving
For the blessings received from above,
Our minutes wouldn't be wasted
But filled with inspiring love.

Life has a special purpose,
We each have a job to do,
We've no reason to catch ourselves loafing,
Could this be said of you?

YOUR BOOK OF LIFE

Another book has been written
And placed upon the shelf –
In the Library up in Heaven,
The author was yourself.
It's been added to the volume,
Which is call "The Book of Life,"
And each book contains twelve chapters
Of how you've lived with strife.
The index is full of topics
Such as peace and joy and love,
And it's how you've handled all of these
That's been recorded up above.
Now it's easy for the Reader
To open the book and see,
Whether your life's been fully lived
According to the Almighty.

But the book you just wrote,
The lids have been closed
And placed upon the shelf
Waiting to be reopened when
You stand before God by yourself.
The mistakes which you've made,
Let's hope were erased,
But a smudge has been left on the page,
And it's easy for the Reader to see by this,
That you've slipped sometimes with rage.

But somehow, let's hope, the index will show,
That you haven't completely failed,
As you tried to live a life from sin,
Redeemed by Christ who was nailed.

1969 VACATION MEMORIES

When I left on vacation
My purse was so full,
And I knew coming home,
Earthly goods I would pull.
So I cleaned out my trunk
And made room for the things
That I'd selfishly buy
In this world that rings.

But now that I'm home
And have cleaned out my trunk,
I can joyously say –
All my riches have sunk.
My trunk was o'erflowing
With the kind little deeds,
Given so generously
By the friends which I need.

So I started unloading
My luggage at last,
Recalling so vivid
The moments that have passed,
Filled with encouragement
For the days that are ahead,
Assuring me fully
I have nothing to dread.

Telling me over
And over again,
There are still people walking
Where our forefathers have been.
Then closing the trunk,
I paused with Thanksgiving –
Knowing and realizing
There are still people living...

A good Christian Life
And are willing to lend
A little encouragement
To a weary friend.

SUBMISSION

Swaying reeds within the fields
That swiftly bend with force,
Just seem to yield to a command
That's from a higher source.

Thus should our lives be like the reeds,
Willing to sway and bend,
Humbly submitting to His will,
Regardless what He sends.

Without resistance – gentle, meek,
Swaying and pliable,
As we bow low and sweep back up
With grace — controllable.

For in so doing we have learned
How to abase — abound,
Which in return produces fields
Of beauty all around.

Reeds along Logan's Ridge, Cleveland, GA

DADDY'S BARN

Daddy's old barn all tattered and torn,
No longer stand today,
Gone are the boards and rusty old nails –
It has fallen away.

Gone are the holes and gone are the knots,
Gone are the rotten beams,
Gone are the posts and gone are the worms,
But something's left, it seems.

For nothing can take the memories,
Or the wonderful smell,
Of all the meat that was cut and cured
By those who cannot tell...

How they would mix up the recipe,
And rub it on the meat,
Then cut and cure, whatever the need,
Until 'twas time to eat.

Or how the family sat around
The table spread so grand,
Beef and pork, from Daddy's old barn,
All from this good old land.

When times were hard and merely a crumb,
Out of the old barn came,
There always was more than enough to share
To any who were lame.

Yes, time moves on and Daddy's old barn,
No longer stands today,
But nothing can take the memories –
They're in our hearts to stay.

MEMORIES

We reach across the many miles,
While time unfolds a special smile —
For just a little while.

We reminisce old time, old scenes,
That filled our lives with radiant beams —
That seem to brightly gleam.

How sweet it was on Sunday morn,
To worship God, see lives reborn —
With Christ — no more forlorn.

Picnics and singings, lots of fun,
With laughter that was never done —
Reflect each memory won.

Moments to share and not forget,
With those we've loved and often met —
Without a fear or fret.

A broken heart where scar tissue,
Mended with time, to strength that's new —
Though battles have been few.

So much to love, so much to hold,
So much, it seems as one grows old —
To keep — and yet be told.

For memories are a priceless gift,
Of treasured thought that somehow lift —
The soul — as time flows swift.

INDEX

ACKNOWLEDGMENTS

I never cease to be amazed at how God works. He is miraculous in all of His ways. His thoughts and ways are much higher than mine, and this I acknowledge. Without Him, these lines could have never been penned and without Him I could have done nothing.

Tom, my beloved husband, also needs to be acknowledged in many ways. Early in our marriage he would pick up a poem I had lying around and he would literally tear it apart. This didn't set very well until I began to understand that he was just helping me with constructive criticism. After I reckonized this, he began helping more and more by giving me ideas and filling me with inspirational thoughts. He has been a kind help-meet, a loyal husband and he is my best friend.

Our daughters, Laura and Carla, along with their husbands, Dean and Ryan, have encouraged us to finish this work. Laura has spent many hours helping to edit and format the book. Without her knowledge this work would have been impossible. Without Carla's "Go MaMa Go" phone calls and her cheering me on, this work would have been impossible. Thank you for all your encouragement and for being a strong family – you helped make this happen.

Our grandchildren, Sheri' and Jeff along with LoriAnn and Logan are in total awe that Grandma is writing a book. But even their amazement has been a source of encouragement, because after Grandma's life is finished on this earth, hopefully this book will live on for them.

A special couple and very dear friends of ours, Dr. H. D. and Patricia Williams of Cleveland, Ga., have been great sources of help in accomplishing this book. Their wisdom and counsel have blessed us. Denny asked me to compile all my writings because he wanted to publish them. I was astonished! This was a dream! The more I worked the more fun I had! Patricia helped me with grammar, punctuation and even ideas. A great big acknowledgment and thank you --- without you this would have been impossible.

I have a dear friend, Kaye Bryan, on Logan's Ridge in Cleveland, Ga. She has been an encourager ever since we first met. She is a friend that I can laugh or cry with. She just understands. Her inspiration and helpfulness has been a great source of encouragement – and this I acknowledge.

Last but not least are two very special friends of mine – Judy Landes of New Carlise, Ohio and Janet Rumble of Modesto, California. I have known Judy since we were fourteen years old. Janet was one of the first that I became friends with after I married Tom and moved to California. I consider both of these girls my bosom friends. They are heart to heart and hand in hand friends. All three of us are great friends and we have shared lots of special moments together. We've laughed together, cried together, sang together and prayed together. These girls have touched my life – and this I acknowledge.

BIOGRAPHY

In 1949, a "Gift from God" was given to a typical Pennsylvania Dutch German family. Early on, community, family, fellowship and Spirit molded this little girl into a woman of the Lord she now is. Accepting Christ and baptism in 1968 was no burdensome decision. Direction in life was given by church heritage rooted solidly in the love for Christ, traced ultimately to the foot of the cross.

I have been allowed to share this "Gift from God" since 1971 with all those with whom we come in contact, from Pennsylvania hills, to California shores and beyond. For this I am eternally grateful. Betty is my companion, best friend, help meet and love of my life, a fit compliment to our love for the Lord, fellowship and family.

Hand in hand we walk together, as we now share the good things of God the Spirit has given Betty to pass on ... from us to you ... "from faith to faith." Rom. 1:17

"To God be the Glory"
Tom Eller

St Matthew 25:41 "Two women shall be grinding at the mill; the one shall be taken, and the other left."

Numbers 11:8 "And the people went about, and gathered it, and ground it in mills, or beat it in a mortar, and baked it in pans, and made cakes of it: and the taste of it was as the taste of fresh oil."

Printed in the United States
148068LV00003B/5/P

9 780982 223031